BISMILLAH KHAN

BISMILLAH KHAN

The Shehnai Maestro

Neeraja Poddar

Revised Edition

Published by
Rupa Publications India Pvt. Ltd. 2015
7/16, Ansari Road, Daryaganj
New Delhi 110002

Sales centres:
Allahabad   Bengaluru   Chennai
Hyderabad   Jaipur   Kathmandu
Kolkata   Mumbai

Edition copyright © Rupa Publications India Pvt. Ltd. 2004, 2015

Text copyright © Neeraja Poddar 2004, 2015

All rights reserved.
No part of this publication may be reproduced, transmitted,
or stored in a retrieval system, in any form or by any means, electronic,
mechanical, photocopying, recording or otherwise, without the prior
permission of the publisher.

The views and opinions expressed in this book are the author's own and
the facts are as reported by her which have been verified to the extent
possible, and the publishers are not in any way liable for the same.

ISBN: 978-81-291-3670-1

First impression 2015

10 9 8 7 6 5 4 3 2 1

The moral right of the author has been asserted.

Typeset by Ninestars Information Technologies Ltd, Chennai

Printed at : Aarvee Printers Pvt. Ltd. New Delhi

This book is sold subject to the condition that it shall not, by way
of trade or otherwise, be lent, resold, hired out, or otherwise
circulated, without the publisher's prior consent, in any form
of binding or cover other than that in which it is published.

CONTENTS

Introduction	7
Kashi	8
Guru-Shishya Parampara	12
Religion and Spirituality	22
A Humble and Sensitive Artist	25
A Simple Man	28
Awards and Recognition	32
Conclusion	44
Forefathers of Ustad Bismillah Khan	47
Landmarks	48
References	50

INTRODUCTION

Cervantes said, 'Where there is music, there can be no evil'. The *shehnai* is one such instrument, a *mangala vadya* whose melodious sound dispels all evil. Earlier, the *shehnai* player would be heard and not seen. At weddings, temples and ceremonial occasions, he would sit in the *naubatkhaana* and play his instrument, invisible to the eyes of those attending the ceremonies. But now the *shehnai* has emerged from behind the *purdah*, the veil has been dropped and it is seen proud and glorious in the very midst of listeners it hid its face from before. It has become a favourite with many discerning enthusiasts of Indian classical music and has attained worldwide fame. One man's efforts are responsible to a great extent for giving the *shehnai* its world renowned status. It is a name that has become synonymous with the instrument itself. He is arguably the greatest *shehnai-vadak* of all times, Ustad Bismillah Khan.

KASHI

The *shehnai* wizard, Ustad Bismillah Khan, was born on a beautiful spring day in Dumraon, Bihar where his forefathers were renowned *shehnai* players of the court. His childhood name was Kamruddin, rhyming with his elder brother's name, Shamsuddin. Bismillah is another name for Allah, and indeed, young Bismillah grew up to be a gift from the heavens for every music lover. When he was just five or six years old, his mother took him to Kashi (modern Benaras) to her brother's home. Bill Aitkin once said about Kashi: 'The milieu of saints, frauds, fakirs, *goondas*, mystics and misfits reminds one that just as India is the world in one country, so Kashi is India on a post card'.

Kashi literally means 'that which shines'.

Previously Benaras was intended to be in the shape of a chariot but it resembles a conch. The conch forms an integral part of Hindu religious ceremonies and is

BISMILLAH KHAN • 9

Kashi Ghat

also one of the oldest wind instruments (the *shehnai* also belongs to the same category).

There is something so magical about Benaras. From the street vendors, the rickshaws and the narrow lanes to the breathtaking temples and the banks of Ganga where hundreds of devotees immerse themselves in the holy waters everyday—all these scenes have captured the imagination of people the world over. Who can help but not be moved while sitting on the banks of Ganga, the river that has the power to wash away all our sins? Who would not be inspired in a place that has been the seat of learning from time immemorial? Benaras has been the hub of Indian music from the olden days and has produced some of its greatest exponents including Girija Devi, Pandit Kishan Maharaj and Pandit Ravi Shankar. Dr. Sushil Kumar Choubey believes that the legendary Tansen was also born here. Even if this is just a myth, the living legend Bismillah Khan certainly lives here and has perfected his musical talents on the banks of this holy river. So deep-rooted is his attachment to this ancient city that he has turned down many lucrative offers inviting him abroad, including one that promised him a replica of Benaras in the USA. He rejected it by saying, 'You will not be able to take my Ganga there.' In his own words 'I say with great happiness and pride that a person who lives in Kashi lives in Heaven.'

He has navigated its narrow lanes as a child, he has sat on the banks of the Ganga here playing his *shehnai* for the pleasure of the holy river, he has been a part of its Muharram processions and has walked through the streets with his magical pipe pressed to his lips, it is the home of his guru and the home of his own family and has been witness to all his success. The air here will always whisper his name and carry through its streets and on its *ghats* the tunes he has played so lovingly in its temples. Benaras has become an integral part of him and judging from his popularity it would seem that he has received the blessings and love of the holy city. He cannot bear to be parted from it, for he cannot live without the Ganga's pure waters at his doorstep, and precisely for this reason he has not pursued a career abroad like so many of his contemporaries.

GURU-SHISHYA PARAMPARA

In the heavenly city of Benaras, Ustad Bismillah Khan learnt to play the *shehnai* under the able tutelage of his maternal uncle, Alibux Khan Saheb. Later he became the student of Lucknow's Ahmed Hussain Khan and Gwalior's famous harmonium exponent Laxmanprasadji (student of Ganpatrao Bhaiya Saheb and nephew of Kashi's Sri Killu Bahadur). Traditionally, learning to play a musical instrument in India did not involve attending routine classes at a school or an institution. It did not imply enrolling for a fixed number of years as a student or payment of tuition fees. The tradition of learning music was embodied in the *guru-shishya parampara*, a relationship of close contact between the teacher and the pupil, where the students lived in the house of the teacher. They not only learnt about Indian classical music but also imbibed the lifestyle, customs and attitudes of the teacher and evolved their own personality accordingly.

The students showed the utmost respect for the teacher and submitted themselves at the feet of the guru. The guru made the students do *riyaaz* and imparted to them intricate knowledge of the *ragas*. His word was law and students obeyed him without question. In Indian tradition, the guru has always held a position comparable to the gods. The *guru-shishya parampara* continues to thrive in many parts of the country, it has nurtured Indian classical music from time immemorial, and to a great extent, is responsible for its continuity. It has kept the melody flowing over centuries—eternally—like the water of the Ganga.

As a boy, young Bismillah did not enjoy studying. He was more interested in playing with marbles and listening to his uncle play the *shehnai*. On the bank of the eternal river, at the Balaji temple, young Bismillah would watch his *Mamu* (maternal uncle) Alibux Khan Saheb do *riyaaz* for four or five hours in the morning. Bismillah would get so lost in the haunting melody that he would forget about hunger and thirst. The spell would be broken only when his *Mamu* stopped playing, suddenly becoming aware that his young nephew must be starving. Curious about his uncle's chosen venue for *riyaaz*, young Bismillah asked him why he did not practise at home. His *Mamu*  told him that he would understand when he was older. One day, Bismillah asked, from when would he be allowed to start playing, and from the very next moment Bismillah's training began.

Initially, young Bismillah practised for half an hour a day and this slowly increased to six hours. His uncle was a strict taskmaster and a perfectionist who drove him hard. Bismillah also realised that producing melodious sounds from the simple looking double reed instrument was not easy. The sweet melodies of his uncle's *shehnai* were the result of many years of strict *riyaaz*. He practised hard, paying no heed to the jeers of his family members when he was tuneless.

Ustadji's father in Dumraon came from a long line of *shehnai* players and young Bismillah was eager to impress his family with his newly acquired skill when he visited them. One day, while playing for his grandfather, he was admonished for playing like a kitten. His grandfather reminded him of his glorious lineage and asked him to roar like a lion. The old man took up his grandson's *shehnai* and the instrument produced sounds that it never had before. The thunderous and overpowering music emanating from the *shehnai* amazed Bismillah and he resolved to learn the secret behind his grandfather's extraordinary power and volume. His grandfather explained that credit should go to his robust health and Bismillah realised that he too needed to be conscious about his habits. Immediately, he began to regulate his diet and embarked on a regular exercise regimen. These changes made a lot of difference and within a week Bismillah noticed an improvement in his breathing techniques.

Bismillah vowed to combine the sweetness of his *Mamu's* playing with the command and strength of his grandfather's. The journey was a difficult one but the earnest young boy never gave up. His perseverance paid off and he was allowed to practise in the Balaji temple, where as a child, he had heard his uncle practising. For young Bismillah, this meant that his guru was satisfied with his progress. Without his teacher's permission, Bismillah would never have dreamt of playing at the temple. Such discipline and respect constitute the foundation of the *guru-shishya parampara* and are strictly followed by its adherents even today.

Ustadji himself is a staunch supporter of the *guru-shishya parampara*, since the intricacies of the *shehnai* were taught to him in accordance to this tradition. He asserts its significance in the modern age of online learning and

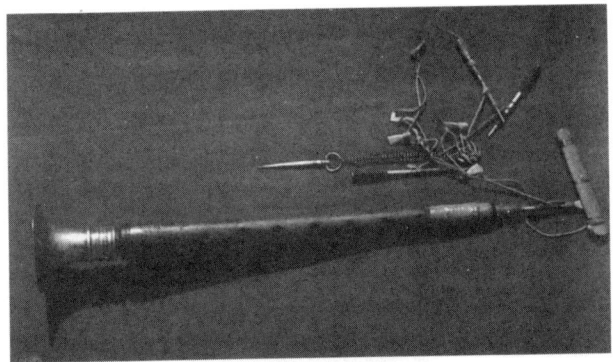

Shehnai

greatly regrets its diminishing importance. He feels that the musicians of today prefer regular schools to *sadhana* with their gurus. In this super fast age, even musicians want instant results and do not have any patience. 'The days of *adab* (old world manner) are gone,' he says, '…the great old masters who did their penance—Fayyaz Khan, Abdul Karim Khan, Onkar Nath—died poor. No one knows about their sacrifices. Consider Swami Haridas. He produced Tansen. But no one knows Swami Haridas. They had no time for their own lives, no time for their families, their children'. Ustadji feels that musicians nowadays lack the stamina and the patience to do real *riyaaz*.

The ability to obliterate the self is gone, the sense of sacrifice is missing. 'You have to get up before sunrise

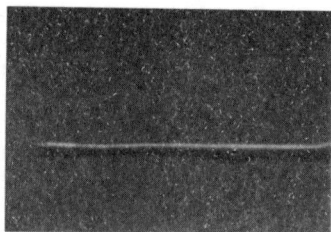

Pyala, Khazana, Nali

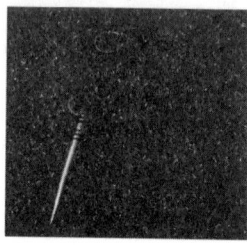

on freezing mornings, offer *namaaz*, go to the *mandir*, and begin practice. These days musicians want to rise at 10 am to go to music schools. Which music school has produced a Fayyaz or an Abdul Karim Khan? I say, leave those schools *aur aao maidan mein* (and come out into the battlefield).' Trial by fire is his norm. 'But you have to have the discipline and the tenacity.' He is willing to commit himself to a serious and committed *shishya* who is ready to imbibe whatever the *guru* has to offer. "He must find the time for his own *tapasya* (penance). I remember the time when I was a boy and often my guru, tired from the day's activities, would retire at 4 am. I would be awake. I had been waiting for him. I used to go to his bedroom and begin pressing his tired feet. He would look at me and would know what I wanted. He would shake off his slumber and come alive. He would give me his *shehnai* and tell me: "all right son, start playing."'

Indian classical music regrets that Ustadji has found only one worthy *shishya*, Jagdish Prasad Qamar, who hails from a simple villager's family although Qamar's father Shree Deepchand was a well-known *naferi* (variety of the *shehnai*) player in Delhi. He heard Ustad Bismillah Khan playing his magical *shehnai* and the desire to become his student was born. Soon, the ten-year old Jagdish came to live in Kashi in 1946.

The *guru-shishya parampara* was adhered to strictly and the relationship between Ustadji and his pupil was reminiscent of the relationship that the young Bismillah had shared with his *Mamu*. Jagdishji's guru was a hard taskmaster, and his patience and endurance were sorely tested before Ustadji started paying any attention to him. Ustadji would ask his eager *shishya* to stay awake until he came to teach him and Jagdish would willingly comply. Late at night, after everyone else had retired, Ustadji would tell him that he was going upstairs and would play a tune which Jagdish was expected to repeat from

Bismillah Khan with Pandit Ravi Shankar

downstairs. The *shishya* could never imitate the guru flawlessly but this did not anger Ustadji and he was more pleased with Jagdish's devotion and earnestness.

Shehnai has remainded a male-dominated art form so far. Jagdishji's daughter, Bageshwari is the world's first and probably only female *shehnai* player. She came to Ustadji in 1989 and has learnt from him. Ustadji comes from a conservative family where women were kept in *purdah* but he does not discriminate between the sexes and teaches anyone who is willing and sincere. He believes, 'More women should play the *shehnai*. It is not that women cannot play. Unless they start practising they will never learn. With the right amount of *riyaaz*, everything is possible.'

RELIGION AND SPIRITUALITY

The famous Vishwanath temple of Kashi is situated in a maze of narrow lanes near the highly populated Muslim locality of the town. Aurangzeb had destroyed the earlier temple in 1669 and Ahalya Bai built the present one in 1777. The Shivalinga has a crack in it and the locals believe that Lord Shiva's heavenly consort, Parvati, attached herself to him along the crack. The deity would earlier be woken up by the sweet tunes of the *shehnai* played by renowned musicians, but now only recorded *shehnai* music is played.

Alibux Khan Saheb had been the official *shehnai vadak* at the Vishwanath temple. It would seem contradictory that a Muslim should be the *shehnai vadak* at a Hindu temple. But it was never a spiritual dilemma for Alibux Khan Saheb and Ustadji has imbibed the same spirit. He is a devout Shia but is also a devotee of Saraswati, the Hindu goddess of learning and music. At the age of twelve, Ustadji received a sign that his *sadhana* had been rewarded. Alibux Khan Saheb had been doing *riyaaz* at the temple of Balaji at Panch-ganga Ghat, Kashi for eighteen years and asked his nephew to do the same. Ustadji recalls: 'I would begin my *riyaaz* at the *mandir* at 7 pm and end at 11 pm, during which time I usually played four ragas. After a year and half, *Mamu* told me, "If you see anything, just don't talk about it." One night as I was playing, and was deep in meditation, I smelt something. It was an indescribable scent, something like sandalwood and jasmine and incense. I thought it was the aroma of the Ganga. But the scent got more powerful. I opened my eyes. I still get goosebumps when I remember this incident—when I opened my eyes, there was Balaji standing right next to me, *kamandal* in hand, exactly as he is depicted in the pictures. My door was locked from inside. Nobody was allowed to enter when I did my *riyaaz*. He said "Play, son". But I was in cold sweat. I stopped playing.'

'He smiled, and disappeared. I unlocked the door. I thought a fakir may have come in. I took a lantern and searched all the streets. They were empty. I ran home, ate quickly and went to sleep. *Mamu* had understood what had happened. But he teased me, pretending he knew nothing. But I blurted out the experience and he slapped me because he had asked me earlier not to talk about anything that might happen to me. Then he kissed me and asked me to go and buy vegetables. *Mamu* always told me "never look back, keep going forward." Even now I go to Balaji's Mandir alone at night and play all by myself. When I play before others, in my heart I am listening to my gurus. In my heart, they clap for me at the appropriate time.'

Ustad Bismillah Khan is deeply religious. Every year, on the eighth day of Muharram, this devout Shia does not raise his *shehnai* to his lips unless he has offered namaaz before sunrise. He has a special *shehnai* made of silver that he plays during Muharram. For the Shias, music is *haraam* (taboo) and yet this pious Shia says: 'Music, *sur*, namaaz. It is the same thing. We reach Allah in different ways… If music is *haraam* then why has it reached such heights? Why does it make me soar towards Heaven? The religion of music is one. All others are different… my namaaz is the seven *shuddh* and five *komal surs*…'

It would seem that Ustadji is flouting the dictates of his accepted faith. But if he is not a true Muslim then who is? He observes the thirty days of *roza* and salutes the *Nabi* (the prophet). In accordance with the teachings of Islam, he does not eat pork, despises alcohol, is not promiscuous and gives alms to the poor. Very few people nowadays follow their religion so correctly and scrupulously and they should be careful before they point accusing fingers at this devout man.

A HUMBLE AND SENSITIVE ARTIST

Ustadji began his career playing with Ali Bux Khan Saheb. In the beginning of his life he had also played with his brother Shamsuddin Khan. Both brothers were expert players, but Ustadji's superior talent was obvious from an early age and he outshone his brother easily. However, being the younger of the two, Ustadji was filled with a deep sense of respect and humility and did not want to insult his elder brother by overshadowing him. 'He was my elder brother, it was not proper for me to play better than him.' Therefore, Ustadji always restrained himself when they played together. He lost his brother early in life and it took great determination on his part to start playing again.

Ustadji exhibits the same sensitivity and humility in all aspects of his music and life. He shows tremendous respect for the other artists he performs with, even if they are many

Playing with his brother Shamsuddin at a wedding, Bismillah is on the left

years younger than him. He never tries to outplay them and always retains his humility and modesty. Ustadji is respected and loved by the entire music fraternity. Artists long for an opportunity to play with him.

Girija Devi has said, 'He is like my older brother. He plays his *shehnai* from the heart... Like his innocent smile, his *shehnai* is also innocent and melodious. Whenever we have performed together, I have learnt something new and have adopted it in my singing with great feeling.'

Birju Maharaj, the world-renowned Kathak exponent feels grateful for his long and affectionate association with Ustadji. Ustadji is a contemporary of the father and uncle of Birju Maharaj and has seen him as the youngest and most loved child of the family. Even today, whenever they meet, Ustadji embraces him and showers him with fond blessings. Birju Maharaj says, 'He is always an inspiration for me, whether I find him in a concert or in the audience.'

Ustadji shares a bond of close friendship and love with his *shehnai* maker, Durgadas Thakur. Born and brought up in Nasik, Durgadas was trained in the intricacies of wood tuning by his father, guru and guide, the late Damodar Govind Thakur. In 1960, Ustad Bismillah Khan personally approached Damodar Thakur to get a *saaz* made and since then, an unbroken alliance has been established between them.

A SIMPLE MAN

Ustadji's inimitable talent became obvious when he was still very young and his daily routine was strictly monitored by his guru. He could not indulge in play all day long, nor could he just sit back, relax and while away his time. His daily routine consisted of hard work, *riyaaz*, preparation, practice and sacrifice with little opportunity for leisure. But even then, he found time for the silver screen and was a big fan of Sulochana and Madhuri, heart-throbs from the era of silent movies. He would be found in cinema halls, watching them with rapt attention. And although getting into the theatres involved a lot of hardship which included appealing for and collecting money from his family, finding time out from practice, standing in long queues to buy tickets,—he bore all this willingly to see these lovely ladies on screen.

But the woman who became his wife was nothing like these sultry sirens. At the tender age of sixteen, Ustadji

married Muggan Khanam, the daughter of his second *mamu*, Sadique Ali, and they had nine children together. Ustadji has always been a faithful husband and strongly believes that lasciviousness and pleasure-seeking would lead to the downfall of his musical talent. His eldest son, Naiyyar Husain, is a talented *shehnai* player while the youngest one, Nazim, is a *tabla* player.

Ustadji's tryst with the silver screen was not confined to watching films alone. He occasionally obliged his friends and did some work in films as well: he composed the music for the popular song *Dil ka khilauna hai toot gaya* in the film *Goonj Uthi Shehnai* for the late Vijay Bhatt and Shankar Bhatt and he performed in the film *Sanadhi Apanna* for another ardent fan, Vikram Srinivas, a film producer from Madras. Both films were huge successes and Ustadji was flooded with offers. But he was never interested in a career in films.

A modest, humble and god-fearing man, Ustadji could never come to terms with the glamour, bright lights and artificiality of the film world. To this day, he enjoys the relative anonymity he gets in Kashi. Ustadji is a simple man, most comfortable in plain white *kurta-pyjamas*. There are few occasions, for example, during his performances, when he is more formally dressed, say in a *sherwani*. He lives in a simply furnished house in Kashi that is in keeping with his character. Ustadji does not believe in ostentation or excess and there is nothing in his dress or demeanour that would provide a clue about the heights he has attained as a musician. Nor is he fussy about the food he eats and maintains simplicity in food habits as well.

Once, the classical singer Parween Sultanaji met Ustadji in London and found him in a state of despair. The maestro had been put up at a hotel by his organisers and he was afraid to touch the meat there, in case it came from improper sacrifice of animals, which is forbidden for Muslims. Instead of throwing tantrums or acting difficult, Ustadji was surviving on bread alone and had become considerably weak. Immediately, Sultanaji took him and his entire entourage to her hostess's residence, bought the correct meat from a Jewish butcher and cooked for hours to prepare an elaborate meal for them. Ustadji was so touched by her care and thoughtfulness that he showered her with loving blessings.

Some of Ustadji's favourite dishes are preparations with lamb, green vegetables, chutney, *badi,* onions, and *roti* with ghee. Beef, however, is forbidden in his house. He admits that his only 'bad habit' is smoking Wills cigarettes. He enjoys this indulgence with great relish. He prefers travelling by train and within Benares he is happiest when travelling on a cycle rickshaw. Ustadji has traveled all over the world to give concerts but ironically, he hates to fly!

In 1965, Ustadji went to participate in the Edinburgh Festival and the Commonwealth Arts Festival. He was a part of a stellar entourage that included Imrat Khan saheb, Pandit Ravi Shankar, Ali Akbar Khan Saheb, Kishan Maharaj and several others. Ustadji agreed to participate but on one condition—he was willing to begin his journey two months before the show but he refused to fly. It was only after immense persuasion on the part of the Indian Council for Cultural Relations (ICCR) and his wellwishers, and an assurance that he would be allowed to go for *haj* (holy pilgrimage) that he agreed. Today, he flies all over the world but would still prefer to travel by train. That too in second class, where the setting is not elitist and he is not hidden away from humanity, unlike in the first class.

AWARDS AND RECOGNITION

Ustadji's melodious tunes have entranced audiences in Afghanistan, Pakistan, Nepal, Iran, Iraq, Saudi Arabia, Kuwait, UAE, Syria, Jordan, Mauritius, Trinidad, Sri Lanka, Japan, France, Germany, England, USA, Canada, erstwhile Soviet Union, Cuba, Poland, China, the Caribbean Islands, Brazil, Spain, Belgium, Sweden, Switzerland, Italy, Africa, Holland, etc. to name a few. The ICCR sponsored his first trip abroad, which was to Afghanistan, in 1962. King Zair Shah of Afghanistan was so pleased with the maestro that he showered him with praise and valuable gifts. Traditionally in India, the *shehnai* has been played during all festivals and ceremonies. Ustadji's *shehnai*, however, is an international *mangala vadya*. The World Exposition in Montreal, Canada in the year 1967, the Cannes Art Festival in France in 1969, and the World Exposition at Osaka, Japan in 1970 are some of the events that Ustadji has graced. His efforts to bring honour to the instrument he loves, have been recognised worldwide and he has been the recipient of various international awards. He has been bestowed with the most prestigious award from the government of Nepal, while in 1992, a newly built auditorium in Tehran, Iran was named after him. The auditorium, which was originally known as 'Talar-e-Rahman' is now called 'Talar Mosiquee Ustad Bismillah Khan'. The government of USA celebrated his eightieth birthday with great pomp and gaiety in New York in 1995. This heartfelt tribute was organized by the World Music Institute, and was a great honour for any Indian musician.

Ustadji was the first Indian to get an opportunity to perform at the Lincoln Centre, New York City, USA. Staring at a vast, alien audience he was initially unnerved. Then he spotted the renowned sitar maestro Ustad Vilayat Khan and was reassured at the sight of a familiar face. His performance was par excellence and the audience was so overwhelmed by his moving melodies that he had to take seven curtain calls. The exuberant audience begged him to say a few words after being enchanted by the language of his *shehnai*. By this time, Ustadji was exhausted and was craving for his 'cup of tea' since it was not customary here, unlike in India, for the *chai* to be kept on stage. Also Ustadji was at a loss for words because his soul had already been poured

Receiving the Padma Bhushan from President Zakir Hussain

forth through his instrument. There was no room for words thereafter. Why was he being asked to speak? But the clapping continued. The audience had been transported into a different realm by music. They felt as if they had 'soared above the Aonian mount' (Book I, Paradise Lost) and they wanted to hear the voice of their Milton.

BISMILLAH KHAN • 35

Padma Vibhushan

Ustadji started speaking with the traditional *namaskar*. He continued in his mother tongue, disregarding whether or not he was being understood by all present. He asked, 'Why are you making me run so much? I have toiled so long with my instrument before you. Now what's the fun of making me run?' This was greeted by laughter and the applause continued steadily. Ustadji continued in his simple language. 'I beg your pardon now. Let me go. I would like to have some tea now.' Then smiling, he continued, 'In our country, there is a proverb that a wise man talks less. So please do not ask me to speak if you have not missed the wisdom of my music.' More laugher and clapping echoed in the auditorium and in its midst Ustadji left the stage and did not give an eighth curtain call. This simplicity and humility are his trademark and he has never abandoned them, even in the face of such mass adulation. He was scheduled to stay in America for two or three days but the duration got extended to about one and a half months.

The International felicitation has not changed Ustadji as a person and he will always remain the simple man from Benaras who needs his *chai* and has an aversion to flying. Though he might stay abroad for a few months, his heart is always in his motherland. International awards are an honour no doubt, but even greater is the recognition he has received in India.

Ustadji entered the star-studded sky of Indian classical music like a comet and its illumination dazzled the eyes of one and all. His immense talent, recognition and laurels have been part and parcel of his career from the very start. Once when he was about fourteen years old, his *Mamu* was packing to leave for the 'Akhil Bhartiya Sangeet Samaroh' in Allahabad. It was a prestigious conference where eminent musicians from all over the country were coming and Ali Bux Khan Saheb was going to start the proceedings with his auspicious *shehnai*. It was a great honour and the house was buzzing with excitement. But the young Bismillah was distraught. He could not bear to be parted from his guru for even a few days. His despair softened the heart of Ali Bux Khan Saheb and the *shishya* accompanied the guru to Allahabad. Young Bismillah was given an opportunity to play at the conference and was applauded by all the great musicians present. Thereafter he went from strength to strength, improving his technique and acquiring a greater name for himself. His second public performance in Lucknow won him a gold medal. But he came into the limelight after winning three gold medals at the All India Music Conference in Calcutta and was invited to perform for the All India Radio. Many offers for solo performances also came his way and he has never had to look back since then. Honours have been heaped on him including two honorary doctorates. He is a prized artist at concerts as well as with the recording industry, and has cut the highest number of LP records in India.

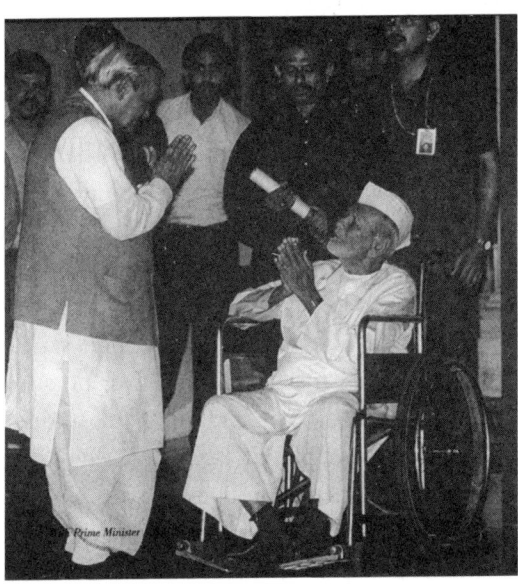

Prime Minister

A rare honour that no other musician can boast of was bestowed on Ustadji some fifty-five years ago. Ustadji had been born into an India that wore the shackles of foreign domination. At an impressionable age, he heard about the atrocities committed by the British, and the bravery and sacrifice of the freedom fighters. As a young man he witnessed his motherland's struggle for independence. The soul of an artist is very sensitive and the entire freedom movement left a deep impact on him.

When India became independent, people all over the country celebrated. On August 15, 1947 every Indian was engaged in some act of jubilation. Some ran out onto the streets in happiness, some offered prayers, some probably cried while others composed patriotic songs to commemorate this joyous occasion. The sensitive musician also celebrated; he was given a rare privilege, something that he cherishes even today. At the request of Jawaharlal Nehru, he became the first Indian to address the nation from the Red Fort while Gandhiji, Azad, Patel and other stalwarts of the freedom struggle sat in the audience. He was the first Indian to deliver a message to a free India. Ustadji did not speak in words but poured forth his heart as he played *raga* Kafi, expressing an entire nation's sentiments through his *shehnai*.

This honour signalled a personal victory for him. His crusade to bring the *shehnai* out of the *naubatkhaana* was

BISMILLAH KHAN • 39

now completely successful, his *shehnai* had touched the heart of every Indian. It had crossed the threshold and entered the arena of Indian classical music in all its glory, and has not looked back since.

This fortunate nation got another opportunity to enjoy a repeat performance on the occasion of fifty years of India's independence on August 15, 1997. Ustadji played the *shehnai* at the Diwan-e-Aam, Red Fort. The programme had been sponsored by the Ministry of Human Resource Development, Government of India. And once again, the nation was moved by his soulful musical tribute. From the first Independence Day to celebrating half a century of independence, the maestro has enjoyed playing on his magical piece of reed.

Today, however, the eighty-six year old musical genius is a worried man, concerned about the state of classical musicians in India. 'During the time of kings and princely patrons, musicians did not have to worry about their livelihood. They were treated royally, and were awarded just as nicely. It was simply a matter of being good at your trade then. The government should do something for the betterment and upliftment of Indian classical musicians,' he adds.

Ustadji is the only musician to have won all four civilian awards presented by the Government of India—the *Padmashree*, the *Padma Bhushan*, the *Padma Vibhushan* and the *Bharat Ratna*. The *Bharat Ratna* is the highest civilian award in the country, and in 2001

it was awarded to Lata Mangeshkar and Ustad Bismillan Khan. Two of India's music icons were nominated for the highest honour, bringing the number of musicians to have won *Bharat Ratnas* to four.

At a colourful function in New Delhi on March 21, President K.R. Narayanan decorated Ustadji and Lata Mangeshkar. Thanking his fans for the award, Ustadji said, 'Music was a gift and gifts were not given easily. I have much more to learn. I want to learn but have no more strength. Age has caught up with me.' He described this honour as an act of the Almighty.

Lata Mangeshkar was asked how she felt about the renowned *shehnai* maestro winning the *Bharat Ratna* with her. She replied, 'Khan Sahib deserves it. In fact, there are so many artists who deserve to be similarly honoured. I am so glad Bismillah Khan Saheb has got the award. I would have liked to see him win it even earlier. I have known and admired him for many years. I have seen him at many concerts. He has also performed at my father's death anniversary. He has visited us at our home. He is a very simple and good-hearted soul.'

Bhaskar Roy from the *Times of India News Service* interviewed Ustadji after the presentation ceremony. 'I never thought I would get the *Bharat Ratna*. Then, when the whole world said I had got it, I said, *chalo maan*

A young Bismillah Khan

liya I have got the highest award,' a visibly moved Ustad Bismillah Khan said.

With the coveted award resting on his chest and his eyes glinting with happiness, the Ustad was in his elements.

Once the formality of the award ceremony was over, he paused in the corridor to answer a few questions. 'All I would like to say is teach your children music, this is Hindustan's richest tradition; even the West is now coming to learn our music,' he said. When asked what did he tell the President, he said, '...play my music in the Rashtrapati Bhavan.'

Though time was short, the Ustad was in a mood to talk. 'There are three ways of doing *riyaaz*: learn music at the *mazhaar*, at the temple or on the banks of the Ganga.' For every sequence, he sang a few lines in a cracked but opulently rich voice. The little crowd that had circled around the wheel chair responded with notes of admiration. 'I am a man from Benares, so I appreciate a little bit of *ras*,' he laughed.

Almost impish like a child, he smiled and said, 'Now please do not ask me questions about politics.' He still practises his *shehnai* but no longer for three and a half hours daily as he once used to. The reason: the kind of Kusum *ghee* his *chapati* used to be soaked in is no longer available. 'The tradition of our classical music should not be weakened,' he pleaded. At the age of eighty-six, Bismillah Khan does not have any more expectations. It has been a long innings marked by fulfilment. This everning marked the epiphany of a rewarding and successful career.

Consciously proud of the Benares *gharana*, his only worry is that Indian classical music has to be saved from the incursions of outlandish influences.

'When I see children swinging to pop, I feel pained,' he remarked.

CONCLUSION

Ustad Bismillah Khan thinks of music as an ode to the gods. It is the only authority he recognises and he lives his life according to the directives of this authority. This does not imply that he is not a devout Shia. He follows the practices of his accepted faith more diligently than the common man does. In religion and in all other aspects of life, Ustadji has never been a blind follower of the norm. He is a Muslim and a true believer of his faith but all his life he has played his *shehnai* in the temples of Benares and is also a devotee of Saraswati. The meat he eats must be properly sacrificed and should meet the requirements of his religion but beef is not permitted inside his house. His favourite disciple is a Hindu and never has Ustadji exhibited even a touch of discrimination against him. Nor does he discriminate between the sexes. Ustadji's life is made up of many such contradictions. His philosophy of life has so many different shades, it has so much depth that if anyone makes an effort to understand it, they will know that they are in the exalted company of a true saint. He is a seer whose vision is not limited by any dogma or narrow-mindedness. Jay Dubhashi writes, 'Ustad Bismillah Khan, the *shehnai* maestro, is the embodiment of Swami Vivekananda's message, "Vedantic mind in Islamic body".' His entire life has been a labour of love. When the sweet strains of the *shehnai* are heard at a concert, rather than only from a *naubatkhana*, we must acknowledge his breadth of vision and his unfailing courage and perseverance to bring honour to the instrument that he loves. He is truly a 'Bharat Ratna', a gem, a prized possession of India and a source of inspiration to artists of the future.

As for his music, words are inadequate to describe its magic. It has the power to transport the listener to a different universe and make him forget the material world. One is reminded of Keats' *Ode to a Nightingale* where the poet finds himself in a dream like state while listening to the nightingale's beautiful song. Ustadji's music produces a similar effect.

P.B. Shelley wrote, 'Music, when soft voices die, vibrates in the memory...'

The music of Bismillah Khan is immortal and will continue to play eternally.

FOREFATHERS OF USTAD BISMILLAH KHAN

Salaar Husain Khan
|
Ustad Husain Bux Khan
|
Ustad Rasool Bux Khan
|
Ustad Paigambar Bux Khan
|
Shamsuddin Khan and Bismillah Khan

LANDMARKS

1916	Born on March 21st in Dumraon, Bihar
1930	Participated in the Akhil Bharatiya Sangeet Samaroh in Allahabad
1932	Married his cousin Muggan Khanam
1935	Participated in the All India Music Conference in Lucknow with Alibux Khan and won the gold medal
1937	Participated in the All India Music Conference in Calcutta and won three gold medals
1956	Awarded the *Rashtrapati Puraskar* from the Kendriya Sangeet Natak Academy
1961	Awarded the *Padmashri* and the National Cultural Organisation's *Shehnai Chakravartee*
1968	Awarded the *Padma Bhushan*

1978 Awarded the *Padma Vibhushan, Deshikottam, Tansen Puraskar* and honorary doctorates from Shantiniketan and Benares Hindu University
1990 Awarded the *Ustad Hafiz Ali Khan Puraskar*
2001 Awarded the *Bharat Ratna*

REFERENCES

'Bismillah Khan-Mystic Union' *India Today*, July 15, 1986.

Ganguly, Rita. 1994. *Bismillah Khan and Benares: The Seat of Shehnai*. Siddhi Books.

Mishra, Kameshwar Nath. 1997. *Kashi ki Sangeet Parampara: Sangeet Jagat ko Kashi ka Yogdan*. Bharat Block Centre.

Krishnaswamy, S. 1965. *Musical Instruments of India*. Publications Division, Ministry of Information and Broadcasting, Government of India.

Mishra, Yatindra. 2001. *Girija*. Vani Prakashan.

Websites

www.chembur.com
www.itcsrs.org
www.screenindia.com

4